D1401315

NEBRASKA

by Jonatha A. Brown

GARETH**STEVENS**
GS
PUBLISHING
A Member of the WRC Media Family of Companies

Please visit our web site at: www.garethstevens.com
For a free color catalog describing Gareth Stevens Publishing's
list of high-quality books and multimedia programs, call
1-800-542-2595 (USA) or 1-800-387-3178 (Canada).
Gareth Stevens Publishing's fax: (414) 332-3567.

Library of Congress Cataloging-in-Publication Data

Brown, Jonatha A.
    Nebraska / Jonatha A. Brown.
      p. cm. — (Portraits of the states)
    Includes bibliographical references and index.
    ISBN-10: 0-8368-4703-2 — ISBN-13: 978-0-8368-4703-1 (lib. bdg.)
    ISBN-10: 0-8368-4720-2 — ISBN-13: 978-0-8368-4720-8 (softcover)
    1. Nebraska—Juvenile literature. I. Title. II. Series.
    F666.3.B69   2007
    978.2—dc22   2005036638

This edition first published in 2007 by
Gareth Stevens Publishing
A Member of the WRC Media Family of Companies
330 West Olive Street, Suite 100
Milwaukee, WI 53212 USA

This edition copyright © 2007 by Gareth Stevens, Inc.

Editorial direction: Mark J. Sachner
Project manager: Jonatha A. Brown
Editor: Catherine Gardner
Art direction and design: Tammy West
Picture research: Diane Laska-Swanke
Indexer: Walter Kronenberg
Production: Jessica Morris and Robert Kraus

Picture credits: Cover, pp. 12, 15, 20, 24, 26 © John Elk III; p. 4 © David
Muench/CORBIS; p. 5 USDA photo by Scott Bauer; p. 6 © Art Today; p. 8
© MPI/Getty Images; p. 9 © Library of Congress; p. 10 © Mora/George
Eastman House/Getty Images; p. 16 University of Nebraska; p. 17 © Spencer
Grant/PhotoEdit; p. 18 © Tom Bean; p. 21 © Tom Bean/CORBIS; p. 22 © Dave
G. Houser/Post-Houserstock/CORBIS; p. 25 © Gibson Stock Photography; p. 27
© Randal L. Kottwitz; p. 28 © Annie Griffiths Belt/CORBIS; p. 29 © Brian
Bahr/Getty Images

Printed in the United States of America

1 2 3 4 5 6 7 8 9 10 09 08 07 06

CONTENTS

Words that are defined in the Glossary appear
in **bold** the first time they are used in the text.

On the Cover: In the 1800s, these huge rocks marked a trail through
Nebraska. The bigger of the two is Courthouse Rock. The other is Jail
Rock.

Introduction

When you think of Nebraska, what comes to mind? Huge ranches with thousands of cattle? Long rows of corn? Tornadoes and dust storms? These things are part of life in Nebraska, but the state also has much more to offer.

Nebraska has stories to tell. It has stories of Native people who followed buffalo across the land. It has stories of explorers who did not know what they would find around the next bend of a river. It has stories of settlers who could not even find wood with which to build their homes.

So, come to Nebraska. Listen to the stories. Learn about life in Nebraska then and now.

Many years ago, thousands of white settlers passed by Eagle Rock on the Oregon Trail.

The state flag of Nebraska.

NEBRASKA FACTS

- Became the 37th U.S. State: March 1, 1867
- Population (2004): 1,747,214
- Capital: Lincoln
- Biggest Cities: Omaha, Lincoln, Bellevue, Grand Island
- Size: 76,872 square miles (199,098 square kilometers)
- Nickname: The Cornhusker State
- State Tree: Cottonwood
- State Flower: Goldenrod
- State Mammal: White-tailed deer
- State Bird: Western meadowlark

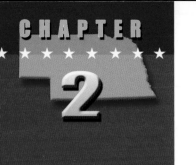

History

Thousands of years ago, Native people came to Nebraska. They followed herds of buffalo, elk, and pronghorns across the land. By the early 1800s, several Native tribes still lived here.

White Explorers and Settlers

Francisco Vásquez de Coronado may have come to this area in 1541. He was a Spanish explorer who was looking for gold. No one is sure whether he got as far north as Nebraska. Even so, the Spanish thought of this region as their land.

In 1682, the French claimed most of the land in the center

FUN FACTS

Many Tribes

Just two hundred years ago, many Native tribes lived in Nebraska. The Omaha and Oto were in the east. The Pawnee lived in what is now central Nebraska. The Sioux and Cheyenne lived in the west. Sometimes, these tribes fought each other for control of the land.

Robert de La Salle claimed this area for France in 1682.

of North America. Their claim included the area we call Nebraska. Soon, French fur traders and trappers began to explore the river valleys. The French set up a trading post on the Missouri River in 1714.

Both Spain and France wanted to control this land. First one country claimed it, then the other. In 1803, the French sold a huge amount of land to the United States. This land sale was called the Louisiana Purchase. The sale included the land in Nebraska. Now, the United States owned this area.

A group of American explorers arrived the next year. Meriwether Lewis and William Clark led the way. They traveled through the eastern part of Nebraska. Before long, more explorers

arrived in the area. Traders and trappers came, too, but most did not settle here. They followed river valleys to the land farther west.

The army built a fort near what is now Omaha in 1819. A trading post was set up at Bellevue four years later. It became the first lasting town built by whites in Nebraska.

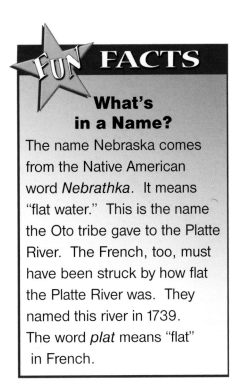

FUN FACTS

What's in a Name?
The name Nebraska comes from the Native American word *Nebrathka*. It means "flat water." This is the name the Oto tribe gave to the Platte River. The French, too, must have been struck by how flat the Platte River was. They named this river in 1739. The word *plat* means "flat" in French.

The Nebraska Territory

In 1834, the U.S. Congress set aside a large area of land for Native Americans to live on. They called it Indian Country. This area included the land that is now in Nebraska. White people were not allowed to

White fur traders set up a trading post at Bellevue in the 1820s. For many years, Bellevue was the most important town in what is now Nebraska. Many people thought it would become the state capital someday, but this did not happen.

IN NEBRASKA'S HISTORY

Stopping along the Trail

Hundreds of thousands of people left the East Coast in the mid-1800s. Families packed their belongings into wooden wagons. They hitched their horses to the wagons and headed west. Most of the **pioneers** followed the Oregon and California Trails. Both of these trails passed through Nebraska. Life on the trail was very hard. Some pioneers did not go all the way west. Some stopped in Nebraska and settled there.

live on this land. Some whites ignored the law and moved in anyway.

In 1854, the land set aside for Native people was made smaller. From some of this land, the Nebraska **Territory** was created. This land was opened for settlement by white people. Many white settlers came to Nebraska to live. Most of them settled on land near the Missouri and Platte Rivers.

8

The U.S. Congress passed a new law in 1862. It was called the Homestead Act. This law gave free land to white settlers who moved to Nebraska. Many people were eager to get free land. They came to Nebraska by the thousands.

A New State

Nebraska became a U.S. state in 1867. At about the same time, a railroad was built. It ran from coast to coast and passed through Nebraska. Now,

By the 1880s, trains were carrying people and goods to and from Nebraska.

IN NEBRASKA'S HISTORY

Natives Against Whites

In the early 1860s, white settlers opened a new trail to Montana. The Bozeman Trail crossed land in Nebraska that belonged to the Sioux people. Led by Chief Red Cloud, the Sioux tried to stop whites from using this trail. They attacked the forts held by the U.S. Army. In the end, the U.S. government tricked Red Cloud into signing a **treaty**. The Army forced the Sioux to move to **reservations** far from their homes.

trains could carry people and goods to and from the state. Trains soon brought more people to Nebraska to live and work.

Droughts hit the state near the end of the 1800s. Without rain, crops dried up and died. Between droughts, millions of grasshoppers invaded the land. They ate the crops and grass. They left almost no grain to harvest and little grass for cattle to eat. Even so, Nebraska kept growing. More than one million people lived here by 1900.

Ups and Downs

In the 1900s, the state went through both good and bad times. Sometimes, rainfall was plentiful and prices were high.

FUN FACTS

A First for Nebraska

The first rodeo in the United States was held in North Platte. It took place in 1882. A big rodeo still takes place in North Platte every summer. Many other cities and towns also host rodeos.

Buffalo Bill Cody was a famous soldier and cowboy. In 1882, he staged the world's first rodeo in North Platte.

These were good times for ranchers and farmers in Nebraska. World War I was one of the good times. During the war, Nebraska helped feed the country and the soldiers who fought in the war overseas.

In the 1920s, prices for crops and goods fell. This was a bad time for farmers and ranchers in Nebraska. Life grew even worse in the 1930s. The whole country was in the midst of the **Great Depression**. Prices fell again, and businesses closed around the country. Many people lost their jobs and their homes. Life was especially hard in Nebraska. A drought hit the state, and more grasshoppers invaded.

Rain fell in the 1940s. Crops began to grow again. World War II brought more

Famous People of Nebraska

Dick Cheney

Born: January 30, 1941, Lincoln, Nebraska

Richard B. Cheney was born in Nebraska. He grew up in Wyoming and married his wife, Lynne, in 1964. Cheney has worked for four U.S. presidents. He started working for President Richard Nixon in 1969. Next, he worked for Gerald Ford and then George H.W. Bush, as well. In 2000, George W. Bush chose Cheney to be his running mate. He and Bush won the election. Cheney became the vice president of the United States in 2001. He and George W. Bush were reelected in 2004.

demand for beef and grain, so prices rose. Once again, life got better for Nebraska's farmers and ranchers.

In the late 1930s, oil was discovered here. It became an important source of money for the people of Nebraska.

Prairies still cover parts of the state. This prairie in the west is protected by law.

Nebraska Today

Big companies started buying family farms in Nebraska during the late 1900s. In 1982, the state passed a law to help save family farms. The law kept big companies from buying farmland in the state. Today, many of the families in Nebraska still live and work on their own farms.

IN NEBRASKA'S HISTORY

Water for the Fields

For many years, droughts caused crops to die in Nebraska. In the late 1930s, the U.S. government set up programs to help solve this problem. Dams were built across rivers, and lakes formed behind the dams. The water in the lakes was used to make electric power and to **irrigate** farm fields. Long ditches carried water to farms. Special equipment spread the water over the fields. Now, the farmers of this state had the water they needed.

Time Line

1682	France claims a large area in the middle of North America; Nebraska is included.
1803	The United States buys the Nebraska area in the Louisiana Purchase.
1823	Bellevue becomes the first long-lasting white settlement in Nebraska.
1834	The U.S. Congress sets aside land in this area for Native Americans.
1854	The Nebraska Territory is created.
1867	Nebraska becomes the thirty-seventh U.S. state.
1883	Women in Nebraska are allowed to vote in some elections.
1917–1918	Nebraska helps the United States fight World War I.
1930s	Nebraska suffers through the Great Depression.
1941–1945	The people of Nebraska help the United States fight World War II.
1974	Gerald Ford becomes U.S. president.
1982	Nebraskans pass a law that prevents large companies from buying farms.
2001	Dick Cheney becomes U.S. vice president.

People

Nebraska is a fairly large state in land area. But it does not have a large **population**. It is home to fewer than two million people. The people are not spread evenly around the state. Most of them live in cities near the eastern border.

People, Then and Now

In the late 1800s, thousands of settlers came to Nebraska. The population of the state grew very quickly. The coming of railroads partly caused this fast growth.

Hispanics

This chart shows the different racial backgrounds of people in Nebraska. In the 2000 U.S. Census, 5.5 percent of the people in Nebraska called themselves Latino or Hispanic. Most of them or their relatives came from places where Spanish is spoken. Hispanics do not appear on this chart because they may come from any racial background.

14

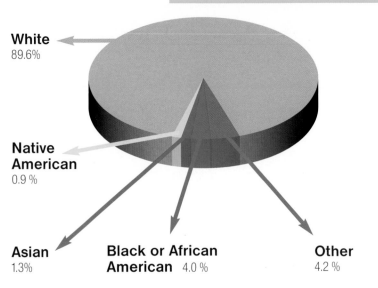

The People of Nebraska

Total Population 1,747,214

White
89.6%

Native
American
0.9 %

Asian
1.3%

Black or African
American   4.0 %

Other
4.2 %

Percentages are based on the 2000 Census.

Omaha rises along the banks of the Missouri River. It is the largest city in Nebraska and an important center for business and shipping.

Trains made travel easier. They brought many settlers to the state in a short time.

In those years, most of the state's newcomers were **immigrants**. Many of these people came to Nebraska from Germany. Others were from Sweden, Ireland, and Britain. People from Russia, Denmark, and some other countries came, too. They brought a mix of **customs** and ideas to their new home.

Today, most of the people who live in the state can still trace their families back to Europe. In fact, nearly nine out of ten Nebraskans are white. African Americans are the next largest group. This group includes about 4 percent of the population. A few thousand Asians live in the state, too. Few Native Americans still make their homes here.

Country and City Folk

For many years, most

Famous People of Nebraska

Susan LaFlesche Picotte

Born: June 17, 1865, Omaha Reservation, Nebraska

Died: September 18, 1915, Walthill, Nebraska

Susan LaFlesche Picotte was the first Native American woman ever to graduate from a medical college. She was born near Macy. Her father was Iron Eye, the last chief of the Omaha people. Her mother was One Woman. Susan learned to speak English when she went to school on the reservation. She was a good student. As a young woman, she went to college on the East Coast. She graduated from medical school in 1889. Susan LaFlesche Picotte returned to the Omaha Reservation to serve as a doctor to her people. She lived and worked there for the rest of her life. A hospital was named for her shortly after she died.

Nebraskans were farmers and ranchers. Today, life is different. Less than one-third of the people live in the country. Most people live in the cities.

Omaha is the largest city, and Lincoln is next in size.

More than one-half of the people in the state live in these cities. Bellevue is the third-largest city. It is much smaller than Omaha and Lincoln. Like those two cities, it is in the eastern part of the state.

Religion and Education

Most people who live in the state are Christian. Of these Christians, Roman Catholics make up the largest group. The state is home to many Lutherans and Methodists, too. Some Jews, Buddhists, Hindus, and Muslims also live here.

Education has long been important to the people of Nebraska. They set up a system of public grade schools in 1855. This was twelve years before Nebraska became a state. In 1875, public high schools were created here.

The state has more than thirty universities and colleges. The largest is the University of Nebraska. More than fifty thousand students attend this school. It has campuses in Lincoln, Omaha, and Kearney.

Omaha is the home of Boys Town. Boys Town started out as a home for boys who had no place to live. Today, many states have Boys Towns and Girls Towns.

CHAPTER 4

The Land

Nebraska is shaped like a rectangle with one corner missing. That missing corner is in the southwestern part of the state. Some people think Nebraska looks like a cooking pot with a short handle. For this reason, the western part of the state is called the Panhandle.

The land in Nebraska is low in the east and higher in the west. In between, the land gradually rises.

The Central Lowland

The state has two natural regions. The Central Lowland is in the east. This region is about 70 to 80 miles (about 110 to 130 km) wide. It covers one-fifth of the state. Most

Each spring, the Platte River offers a quiet resting spot for Sandhill cranes as they fly north.

NEBRASKA

SOUTH DAKOTA

Oglala National Grassland

Niobrara R.

Niobrara R.

Lewis and Clark L.

Royal

Winnebago IR

Elkhorn R.

Omaha IR

Samuel R. McKelvie NF

Agate Fossil Beds NM

Nebraska NF

Wildcat Hills

Scotts Bluff NM

Nebraska NF

North Loup R.

Middle Loup R.

Loup R.

Platte R.

Dissected Till Plains

Missouri R.

IOWA

WYOMING

Chimney Rock NHS

Sand Hills

North Platte R.

L. McConaughy

South Loup R.

Lodgepole Creek

Panorama Pt.

South Platte R.

North Platte

Platte R.

Grand Island

Omaha

Bellevue

Big Blue R.

Lincoln

COLORADO

Frenchman Creek

Kearney

Hastings

Little Blue R.

MO

Harlan County L.

Republican R.

KANSAS

SCALE/KEY

0   50 Miles

0   50 Kilometers

⊘ State Capital

▲ Highest Point

Mountains

N S E W

of Nebraska's people make their homes in this region.

The Central Lowland is an area of gently rolling hills. Thousands of years ago, this land was covered by huge, thick sheets of ice known as **glaciers**. These glaciers melted and left a thick layer of dark, rich soil behind. This soil is very good for farming.

The Great Plains

The other four-fifths of the state lie in the Great Plains region. This land is higher than the land farther east. One interesting part of the plains is the Sand Hills. This area is in the center of the state. It is the largest area of sand dunes in North America. Grasses grow on the dunes and provide good grazing for cattle.

North and west of the Sand Hills is an area called the High Plains. The land is mostly flat here. Rough, rocky ground breaks through in some places. The High Plains is one of the few parts of this state where forests

Major Rivers

Missouri River
2,466 miles (3,968 km) long

Niobrara River
431 miles (694 km) long

Republican River
422 miles (679 km) long

grow. The main trees in this area are pines. A big cliff known as Pine Ridge marks the northern edge of the High Plains. It plunges 1,000 feet (305 meters) to the land far below.

The southwest has hills and canyons. The highest point in Nebraska is found in this part of the state. It is Panorama Point. It rises 5,424 feet (1,653 m) high.

Scott's Bluff is in western Nebraska. From the top of the bluff, you can see far across the prairie.

Waterways

Most of the rivers in the state run east. They flow toward the Missouri River. The Missouri River forms Nebraska's eastern and northeastern borders. The Platte River flows across the state, from west to east. This river is long, but it is too shallow for boats. The Niobrara River crosses the northern part of the state.

More than two thousand lakes dot the land. Most of these lakes are small. Lake McConaughy is the largest of Nebraska's lakes. It was formed when a dam was built on the Platte River.

Fierce Weather

Summers are sizzling hot in Nebraska, and tornadoes sometimes occur. Each year, about forty "twisters" hit the state. Winters are terribly cold, and blizzards can be deadly. Too much and too little rain can be a problem in the state, too. Floods and droughts are common.

FUN FACTS

Sod Houses

Only about 4 percent of the land in Nebraska is forested. The rest is grassland. When the early settlers came, they could not find enough wood to build houses. They cut chunks of prairie grass and dirt out of the ground. These grassy chunks are known as **sod**. They used the sod like bricks. Instead of building wood houses, the pioneers built sod houses.

Economy

Nebraska has long been known as a farming and ranching state. About 93 percent of the land is used for growing crops and raising livestock. Most of the farms are in the east. Ranches are more common farther west.

The top farm product is beef cattle. Pigs, milk cows, sheep, and chickens are also raised here. Livestock bring in about two-thirds of all farm **income**.

Crops are important, too. Corn is the number one crop. Most of the corn raised here is fed to livestock. Wheat, oats, and other grains are raised here, as well. Hay and soybeans are also **major** crops.

Nebraska has long been one of the top beef-producing states in the nation.

Factory and Service Jobs

Much of the meat and grain that is raised in Nebraska is processed here, too. Factory workers make baked goods, packaged meats, cereals, and livestock feeds. At some of the state's factories, workers make equipment for farming and irrigation. Omaha has more factories than any of the other cities in the state. Lincoln has many factories, too. It is home to a center for testing tractors.

Many people in Nebraska have service jobs. Service workers help other people. They work in hospitals, hotels, schools, and many other places.

Insurance is big business in the state, too. Nebraska is home to more than thirty insurance companies.

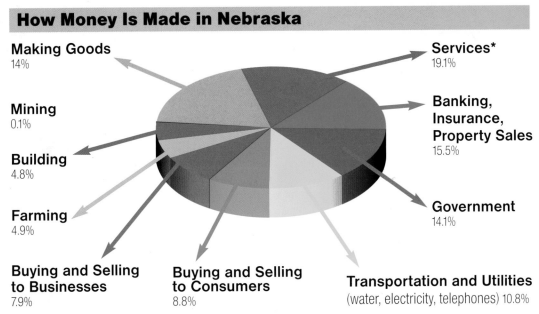

How Money Is Made in Nebraska

Making Goods 14%

Mining 0.1%

Building 4.8%

Farming 4.9%

Buying and Selling to Businesses 7.9%

Buying and Selling to Consumers 8.8%

Transportation and Utilities (water, electricity, telephones) 10.8%

Government 14.1%

Banking, Insurance, Property Sales 15.5%

Services* 19.1%

* Services include jobs in hotels, restaurants, auto repair, medicine, teaching, and entertainment.

CHAPTER 6

Government

Lincoln is the capital city of Nebraska. The state leaders work there. The state government has three parts, called branches. These parts are the executive, legislative, and judicial branches.

Executive Branch

The job of the executive branch is to carry out the state's laws. The leader of this branch is the governor. The lieutenant governor and other state officials help the governor.

The state capitol building is in Lincoln. This tall building is topped by a gold dome.

The governor lives in this mansion in Lincoln. The mansion is open to visitors once each week.

Judicial Branch

Judges and courts make up the judicial branch. Judges and courts may decide whether people who have been **accused of** committing crimes are guilty.

Legislative Branch

The legislature makes laws for the state. Most states have a legislature made up of two parts, or "houses." Nebraska is the only U.S. state that has a legislature with only one house.

Local Governments

Nebraska has ninety-three counties. Most are run by a small group of people. Cities are often led by a mayor or city manager and council. Native tribes have their own governments.

NEBRASKA'S STATE GOVERNMENT

Executive		Legislative		Judicial	
Office	**Length of Term**	**Body**	**Length of Term**	**Court**	**Length of Term**
Governor	4 years	Legislature		Supreme (7 justices)	
Lieutenant Governor	4 years	(49 members)	4 years		3 years, then 6 years
				Appeals (6 judges)	
					3 years, then 6 years

CHAPTER 7

Things to See and Do

Nebraska is full of interesting things to do. In the summer, you can go to a Native American powwow. The powwow in Macy is one of the oldest in the United States. You can see Native dance contests and learn about Native customs.

The Henry Doorly Zoo is in Omaha. It has the largest indoor desert in the world. It has the largest indoor rain forest, too. Ashland is home to the Strategic Air and Space Museum. There, you can see old airplanes and learn about space travel.

Omaha is home to the Henry Doorly Zoo. It is one of the best zoos in the country.

Famous People of Nebraska

Gerald Rudolph Ford

Born: July 14, 1913, Omaha, Nebraska

Gerald Ford was the thirty-eighth president of the United States. He became president in an unusual way. In 1973, he was a member of Congress. Richard M. Nixon was president, and Spiro T. Agnew was vice president. Agnew resigned, so Nixon had to choose a new vice president. He chose Ford. The next year, Nixon resigned. This made Ford president. Ford served for two and one-half years. In 1976, he ran for reelection and was defeated by Jimmy Carter

You can learn about the history of Nebraska all over the state. Many museums have exhibits about pioneer life. In some places, you can still see where the wheels of covered wagons cut ruts into the land!

The Great Outdoors

Nebraska has many state parks. Fort Robinson State Park is in the northwest. It was once an army post on the **frontier**. Today, you

Kool-Aid was invented in Hastings in 1927. Each year in August, Hastings holds a Kool-Aid Days festival to celebrate the city's claim to fame.

can explore old buildings and visit two museums. The park's natural areas are full of wildlife. On your visit, you may see bighorn sheep, pronghorns, and buffalo.

Do you like old bones? If you do, head for Ashfall **Fossil** Beds State Historical Park. This amazing place is near Royal. Here, you will see bones of rhinoceroses,

These rhinoceros bones are ten million years old! You can see lots of fossils like these at the Ashfall Fossil Beds State Historical Park.

Famous People of Nebraska

Malcolm X

Born: May 19, 1925, Omaha, Nebraska

Died: February 21, 1965, New York, New York

Malcolm X was born Malcolm Little. He was an African American who often saw whites treat black people very badly. He had a hard childhood. When he was a young man, he went to jail for robbery. There, he became a **Black Muslim**. After leaving jail, he changed his name to Malcolm X. He became a minister and began speaking in public. Malcolm X spoke about "Black Power" and urged African Americans to take control of their lives. For many years, he thought black people would be better off if they lived apart from whites. He was shot and killed while giving a speech.

DIY EASTER DÉCOR

FRAMED BUNNY WALL ART

YARN-WRAPPED WREATH

FELT CARROT CANVAS ART

Find instructions for these projects and more craft inspiration at **michaels.com/easter**

THANK YOU

Use these coupons to save on your next purchases.

horses, and camels that lived millions of years ago.

Most of the state parks offer hiking and camping. Some of the parks are on lakes, streams, and rivers. They offer places to swim, sail, canoe, and more. If the fish are biting, you can catch catfish, pike, and bass. You can ride horses, too. Pick your mount, swing into the saddle, and hit the trail!

FUN FACTS

Crazy about Football

If you mention sports in Nebraska, most people will want to talk about football. Nebraskans are especially proud of the Cornhuskers. For more than forty years, the Huskers have been one of the best teams in college football. They play for the University of Nebraska.

In 2005, the Nebraska Cornhuskers (in red and white) faced the Michigan Wolverines in the Alamo Bowl. The Cornhuskers came from behind to win the game 32–28.

accused of — blamed for

Black Muslim — a member of a group of African Americans with Islamic religious beliefs

customs — ways of doing things

droughts — long periods of time without rain

fossil — a bone or shell that has turned to stone over thousands of years

frontier — a place that is just starting to be settled

glaciers — huge, thick masses of ice that move across the land over hundreds or thousands of years

Great Depression — a time in the 1930s when many people lost jobs and businesses lost money

immigrants — people who leave one country to live in another country

income — money earned

irrigate — to send water from a river or stream to a field through ditches

major — big, important

pioneers — the first people to settle in an area

population — the number of people who live in a place, such as a state

reservations — lands set aside by the government for a special purpose

sod — dirt that has roots and grass growing in it

territory — an area of land that belongs to a country

treaty — a written agreement

TO FIND OUT MORE

Books

C Is for Cornhusker: A Nebraska Alphabet. Discover America State By State (series). Rajean Luebs Shepherd (Sleeping Bear Press)

Native American Doctor: The Story of Susan LaFlesche Picotte. Jeri Ferris (Sagebrush)

Nebraska. This Land Is Your Land (series). Ann Heinrichs (Compass Point Books)

Nebraska Facts and Symbols. States and Their Symbols (series). Emily McAuliffe (Franklin Watts)

Peeking Prairie Dogs. Pull Ahead Books (series). Christine Zuchora-Walske (Lerner Publications)

Web Sites

America's Story: Buffalo Bill Cody
www.americaslibrary.gov/cgi-bin/page.cgi/aa/cody

Enchanted Learning: Nebraska
www.enchantedlearning.com/usa/states/nebraska/

National Geographic: Nebraska Sand Hills
www.nationalgeographic.com/wildworld/profiles/terrestrial/na/na0809.html

Nebraska for Kids
www.visitnebraska.org/about/kids/

INDEX